FooTroT FlaTs ™

COLLECTOR'S EDITION

Other Footrot Flats titles are:

Footrot Flats Volume 1 1976
Footrot Flats Volume 2 1977
Footrot Flats Volume 3 1978
Footrot Flats Volume 4 1979
Footrot Flats Volume 5 1980
Footrot Flats Volume 6 1981
Footrot Flats Volume 7 1982
Footrot Flats Volume 8 1983
Footrot Flats Volume 9 1984
Footrot Flats Volume 10 1985
Footrot Flats Volume 11 1986
Footrot Flats — Japanese Edition 1986
They've Put Custard With My Bone 1982
The Cry Of The Grey Ghost 1983
Kiddie-Widdies Footrot Flats 1983
I'm Warning You Horse 1984
The Footrot Flats Weekender 1985
Footrot Flats — The Dog's Tail Tale 1986
(Magpie Productions)
The Making Of The Movie 1986
(Magpie Productions)

© *Diogenes Designs Ltd*

ISBN-0-86464-094-3

inprint
NEW ZEALAND

Printed and published by Inprint Ltd,
Eastern Hutt Rd, Taita, Lower Hutt,
New Zealand. The company's registered
office is at 78 Victoria St, Wellington,
New Zealand.

FooTroT FlaTs ™

COLLECTOR'S EDITION

Based on volumes one, two, three & four

BY

Murray Ball.

© MURRAY BALL

SPLUK!

SPLUK!

1

To The NZ Sheepdog—

When I was a young man I worked on my Uncle's farm.

Well, he worked, I played.

It was a time when I was waiting to be selected for the All Blacks. To fill in the time I rounded up sheep.

I stalked with my tongue hanging out and my ears pricked waiting for one to break away from the mob. I would then crash tackle it (they were softer and lacked the fend of my more orthodox opponents). This continued for about 3 weeks.

It was a Saturday morning, I think. I had brought in a large mob and had returned sweaty and bright-eyed to have my head patted. As I stood beside my Uncle, the old huntaway, Wag, rose from where he had been lying in the shade under the macrocarpas and walked over to us.

He looked up into my eyes, raised his hind leg and piddled on my foot.

I think it reflects well on the good nature of this noble breed that he had not done it sooner and had stopped at just urinating.

It must have been insufferable for these master musterers to watch a gangly youth perform this parody of their art.

Footrot Flats is my attempt to say sorry Wag. It is also my tribute to one of the world's minor miracles; the farmer's half-mile hand, the dog on the end of the whistle.

Murray Ball

I gotta hand it to Wal, he isn't pushy. Nope, if there's a bull to be moved, he lets me do it. If someone has to have first taste of Cooch's toad and enunga fritters, he lets me do it. If there's a book to be started and there's footy on television, he lets me do it.

Well, as it happens, he has got just the right joker for the job. I happen to know the Footrot Flat weirdos better than most. I have ridden on, fallen under, been trampled by, rolled over and been butted, kicked, savaged, licked, pecked or hurled by most of them at one time or another. And there is no better way of getting to know a person than to have actually been inside their gumboot, I always think.

So, in the next few pages, I'm going to tell you a bit about the Footrot Flats mob — starting with probably the toughest, most powerful, interesting and yet most modest of them all . . .

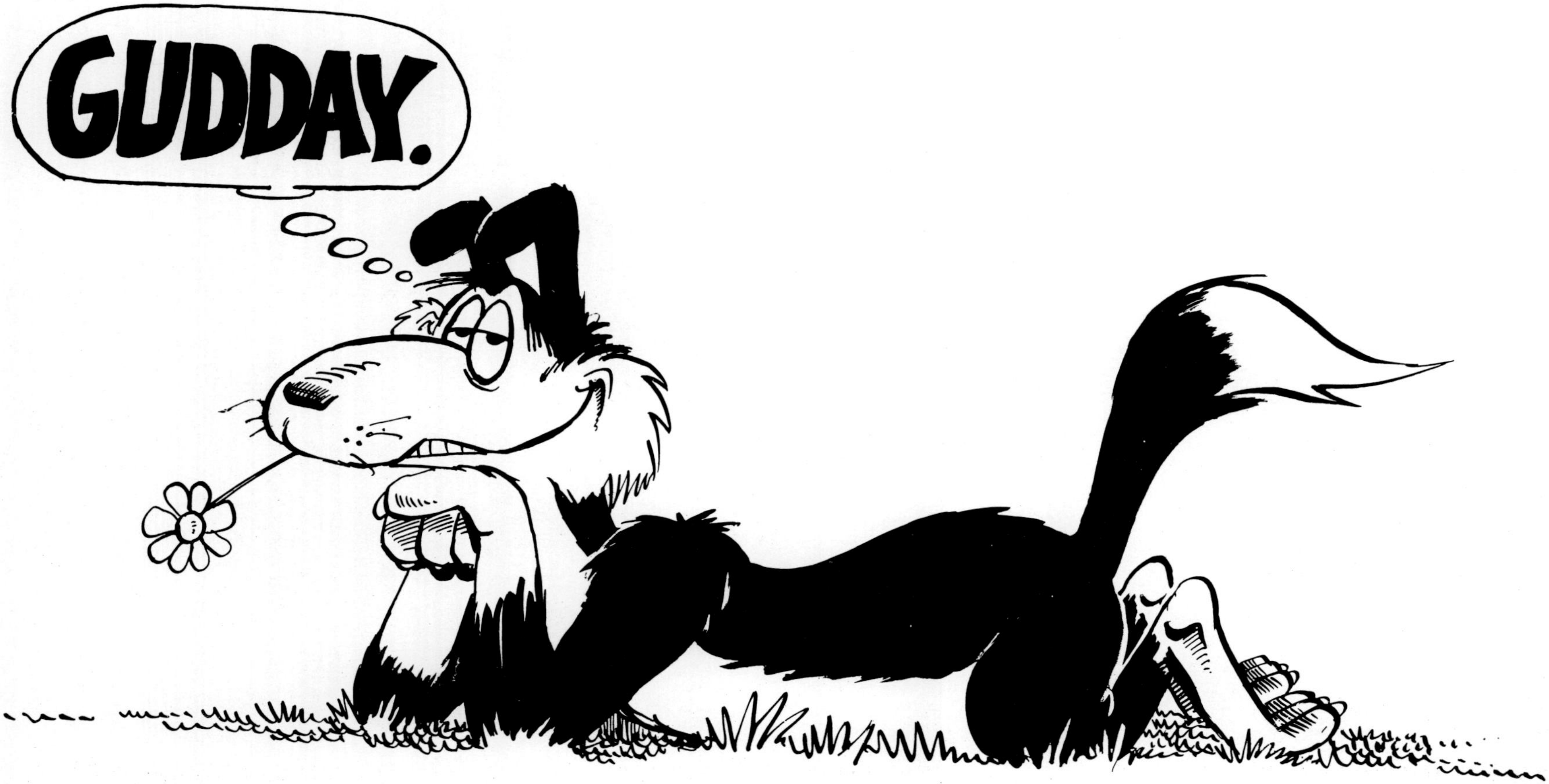
GUDDAY.

The Dog

[A PICTORIAL HISTORY]

Wallace Cadwallader Footrot

Born on 26th January in Northern Manawatu.

Educated at Apiti Primary School and later Foxton Agricultural High, where he excelled at tractor reversing and rooster imitations. Established an outstanding relationship with muscovy ducks—but unfortunately failed completely with geese. Indeed he seemed to have an uncanny knack of irritating them.

He took a full part in all school activities. Displayed a promising right cross during his time in the front row of the 2nd XV, but was unable to transfer this ability to the boxing ring. He rather let the side down during the inter-school championships by throwing in the sponge which knocked the referee's glasses crooked. He was disqualified.

On leaving school, he acquired 400 acres of swamp between the Ureweras and the sea.

He is unmarried, although he has an interest in a certain Darlene (Cheeky) Hobson who works in the Ladies Hairdressers at Raupo (pop. 406).

He is a stalwart of the local rugby football team. He was a moving force in formalising the law that football boots will be worn only when more than 60 percent of both sides has a pair.

A good-humoured fellow who smiles readily. (The last time was when Cooch got his arm caught down a rabbit burrow while trying to rescue a rabbit. He laughed aloud when the rabbit bit Cooch. That was in 1974).

He has relations all over New Zealand. As a matter of fact he got me from his Aunty Dolly in Tauranga. She is a terrible woman. She attended a Royal Garden Party on a trip to London and has never recovered from the honour of treading in Corgi droppings under a Rhododendron bush. Her shoe is kept in a glass box on her television set. She named me.

Cooch Windgrass

Wal's mate, neighbour and right hand man. A beauty bloke — ask any possum, deer, rabbit, magpie or weta. The only joker I know who'd give his Jacky Howe to a slug with a sniffle. He keeps goats and blackberry. He has a cabbage tree growing up through his verandah floor. The roots of a Puriri have pushed his house crooked. You have to climb up the floors in some places and jog down the slope in others.

The most violent act I ever saw him commit, was to spit a codlin moth from his apple out of the window.

Mind you, He's not a vegetarian. He does kill to eat. His eel and puffball stew is an acquired taste, as is his huhu grub, puha and chips.

A native of the 'Flats' — his family owns two thousand acres of swamp, tussock, scrub, forest and mudflat — Wal reckons it's a crime that they don't bulldoze it flat and farm sheep instead of pipis and paua. But I reckon he's got a soft spot for old Cooch — like the rest of us.

He can catch flounder with his bare feet.

Major

Wal's pig dog. Thinks he's a big wheel. Just because he's tough, strong, brave, courageous and brainy, he thinks he's better than the rest of us. Well, I'm going to show him one day. I'm working on being as brainy as him at the moment—and that tells me I shouldn't rush things. But he just better watch it, that's all!

The Turkey

My main enemy. A Bully. And like all bullies, a coward. One day I'm going to stand up to him, grab that red dangly thing on his beak and sock him right between the eyes with it. That'll show him up for the coward he is.

When I get older—after Christmas, maybe . . .

The Goat

Wal got him to keep the grass down. But he doesn't seem to like grass. He seems to prefer to keep the fruit trees, Wal's footy socks and Wal down.

I'm not going to say too much here as the cunning old sod is sharp enough to read it.

9

14

16

Jess

Murray Ball

© 1986 Diogenes Designs Ltd

18

This is my very good friend, Jess.
Jess lives up the Road. At Cooch's Place
to be exact.
She is neat. At certain times of year
She is neat and also VERY INTERESTING!!
She loves and admires me. She has
very good taste... except at certain times
of year...
I think she is what siciatrists would call
schitzophrenic scitsofren skitzo a split
personality. Which is annoying because
just when she becomes VERY INTERESTING.
altho she still loves and admires me she
also loves and admires every other dog in
the district.
She is very liberated. But I ador udor
udder think she is really neat.
P.S. she is offen a one parent family which
is not easy with 10 kids, eh?
She can get really niggly.
Is it my FAULT?!!
well, sometimes...

19

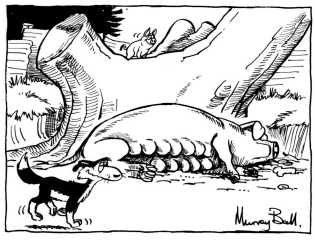

Aunt Dolly

Aunt Dolly (Alleeyus Dolores Footrot. Wal's
aunty who owns a cats Home
in Tauranga)

The most Fowl-mouthed Footrot. She gave me
my name, curse her! May her tongue be
caught in the mincer while she is doing Her
pussy's Din dins and be eaten by a Tom cat
with sharp teeth and Active bowels.

Mind you she'd probably just dab it with
Dettol and pop a sticking plaster on it.

She is tougher than Wal' as tough as the
goat but not as tough as Horse.

As for me, I defy her! I snap my fingers
at her! I laugh in Her face!

But not where she can see me.

32

33

38

39

The Cat Called Horse

© 1986 Diogenes Designs Ltd

Meet ''Horse'' — he's the king of the strays around our place. We call him ''Horse'' because the night he walked through the kitchen door Wal said ''!!!//!**, he's as big as a horse'' and threw his gumboot at him. ''Horse'' swatted it down in mid air and punctured it in half a dozen places with his teeth and then took off with the leg of mutton from the bench. Wal shot after him with the carving knife but trod on one of my chop bones with his bare foot. His Aunty Dolly told him it served him right for persecuting starving animals. Wal said the only starving animal about the place was him. Aunty Dolly refused to give him rhubarb and ice cream for giving her cheek. So, Wal doesn't think much of ''Horse'' — and I agree with him. I intend running the mangy beggar off the place as soon as I meet him with his jaw strapped shut and all his legs in splints.

WAL BOOTIN' HORSE OUT OF THE KITCHEN

HORSE TEARIN' OUT OF THE KITCHEN SCARED OUT OF HIS WITS AND VOWIN' NEVER TO RETURN

47

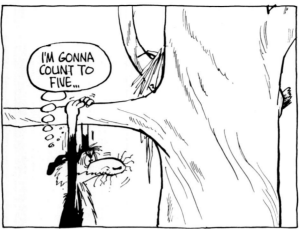

AUNTY DOLLY'S
PHOTO ALBUM

Wallace using fly-spray instead of deodorant before meeting that Darlene Hobson in Raupo on Friday night. ←

That uncouth fellow Cooch Windgrass threatening me with a grilled lamb's tail and tomato sauce at this season's docking. →

51

56

62

THE SECRET WAL' AND

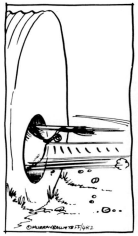

73

74

76

Introducing Janice Pongo Footrot

You may have noticed, during the year, a rotten hard case kid with pony tails and sticky fingers has popped into the picture from time to time. She is "Pongo" Footrot. Wal' has a brother, Rex, who lives in the King Country making pots and breeding kids with sticky fingers and pony tails. The little ones also have heavy naps and bubbles coming out of their noses. But it is this Pongo that comes over for holidays and feeds her dolls my dog biscuits and uses my water tank to hold her parties in. If you have ever tried to sleep on a blanket that has raspberry drop tea spilt on it, you'll know why I hate school holidays.

Wal' is as wet as a shearer's socks with her. She doesn't get in behind when she walks with him, yet I have never seen him bonk her with a bullock bone.

To be fair, she does have a better side to her nature. She has been known to empty her tripe out of the window when unobserved and has several times smuggled calf liver to me concealed up her jersey. But tripe and calf liver bribes cannot make up for bubblegum rubbed in your ears, kids and cuddly toys in your dog-box and having to ride tucked up in her doll's pram with her damn baby's bottle shoved in your mouth.

I have tried scratching fleas into her pram but they seem reluctant to emigrate. Fleas are not fools. I'm afraid we will just have to tolerate her until she gets older and starts getting interested in horses.

Love

The Dog.

79

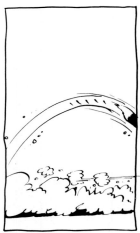

85

92

94

101

Dolores The Sow

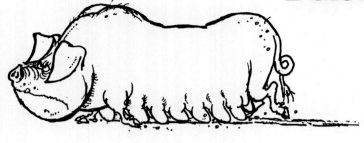

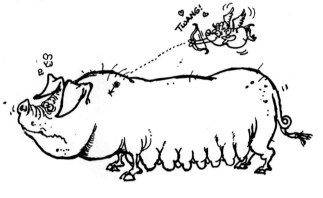

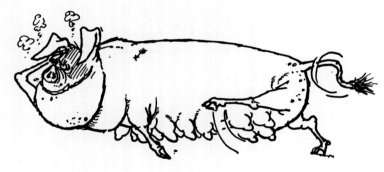

Boris The Boar

106

SWOP!

It's PEW the Magpie!!

Now I'm not sayin' the baby magpie hasn't got a case. I reckon I'd be a bit niggly too if Wal cut down the tree me and me mum were nesting in. But seeing me old man land a whitey on the saw-crazed sod would have gone a long way to making me feel better. But not little PEW the Pied Avenger! No, he has dedicated his life to dogging Wal's footsteps and havin' a bit of the poor beggar every time he exposes a sensitive area. To see young Pew with a good grip on Wal's nostril hairs is enough to make your eyes water. Even after Wal kindly gave Pew to Cooch for his birthday present he didn't get rid of him completely. Pew still invades us from time to time and returns home carryin' a small bundle of under-arm hairs with skin still attached to the roots.

If the little beggar has a weakness it is that being orphaned so young he is always lookin' for a mother figure. He spotted a pie-bald shape in the hayshed the other day. He waddled in with his wings outspread croakin' "Mummy! Mummy!" Well nobody calls it "Mummy" twice. When the feathers had cleared Horse was clawing at a crack in the floorboards and Pew was sitting amongst the cobwebs and rat droppings under the shed lookin' like a startled gooseberry and wondering whether a mother with a sledge-hammer right hook and a liver sausage breath was worth having . . .

WHO SLEW PEW?
"I" said Horse,
"It's PAR for the course,
"I SLEW PEW!"

(Just a little poem I thought I'd pop in. Not true of course. We should BE SO LUCKY!)

SWING!

ZANK!

FLIP!

111

114

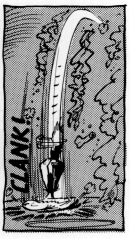

116

BONK! CHONK!

KA-DONK! SPRONG! THUMP!

ARF! ARF! ARF! ARF!

WALLACE! THAT DASHED GOAT IS LOOSE AND AFTER MY WASHING ON THE LINE!

OKAY AUNT', I'LL SEE TO HIM...

THUMP!
WHAM!
BAA-AAAA!
YIKKA YIKKA!
ZONK!
CLONK!
ZUNK!
ZUNK!
ZUNK!

DARN IT WALLACE, I THINK I'D RATHER HAVE THE GOAT!

CHOMP! CHOMP! CHOMP! CHOMP!

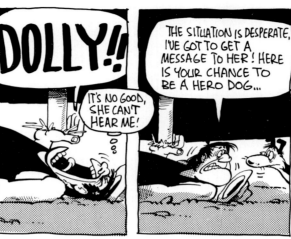

120

Cecil The Ram

Cecil is OLD.

He is so OLD he has seen Wal' wash his footy gear TWICE!!

He was a Top Ram when Being a Top Ram was not concidered to Be an anti-woman put-down... And certainly no one has a greater Respect for the female of the species than Cecil. As he is wont to say in moments of Reverie whilst hiding under the woolshed "Rams come and Rams go – But Ring-crutched ewes go on for ever and ever...and ever...

Some have hinted That he is a... you know... a missogynist. That is a DIRTY LIE! He is just as much a Misterogynist as me or any other normal, decent bloke! It's just that He feels much the same as I Did when the Beef carcass fell out of the Killing tree onto me. i.e. that you can get Too Much of a Good Thing! –

Cec's main ambition now is to Be accepted as the Monk's Mascot in a monastary – or failing that as chief cricket pitch mower at some equally wholesome institution – perhaps a boys boarding School.

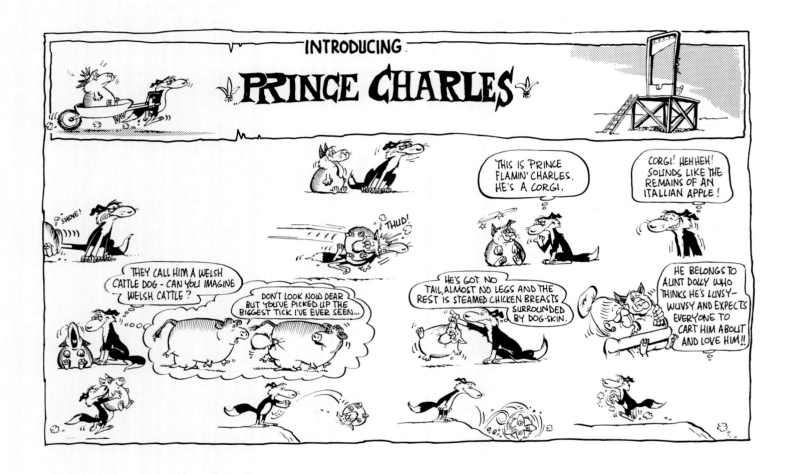

126

128

131

133

134

139

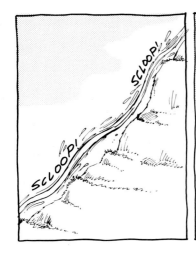

141

Cheeky Hobson

Cheeky Hobson

I honestly cannot understand what Wal' sees in Cheeky Hobson. She has fat, red lips, pink skin, over-weight mammaries, a large bottom, big thighs and lots of blond hair — but only on her head as far as I can make out.

Perhaps he is sorry for her. Be that as it may — she is a THRET!

She owns a beauty saloon in Raupo and slinks around the place exuding Promise-of-Passion Body mist and swarve city sophistication. She drinks Charconray Shardo claret with her fish and chips — the slut!

Wal', as bright a bloke as you would find this side of the letter box, is putty in her hands. But she shall not prevail! If it comes to a choice between her and me he'd rather have a decent, clean liven right-hand bloke than a fat chested blond whose only talent seems to be to sit too close to him and reek like a harem on a hot night.

Eh?

147

148

150

156

© 1987 Diogenes Designs Ltd